ISBN: 978-1-09830-353-2

D0905736

"*Curriculum-driven resources flood today's Christian discipleship market. Many of these resources either minimize or disregard the significant role that evangelistic disciple making plays in discipleship. However, Dr. Anthony Svajda's believes that the Bible is the curriculum of all Christian discipleship and that every discipleship strategy must begin and end with the gospel. In the Text-Driven Discipleship Guide, Svajda disciples both would-be and immature believers by presenting them with the gospel, in order that they may obey the gospel, so they, themselves, may share the gospel and make disciples. Make sure your church is using this excellent resource, which I believe to be our generation's discipleship survival kit.*"

Matt Queen, Associate Professor and L. R. Scarborough Chair of Evangelism ("The Chair of Fire"), Associate Dean of the Roy Fish School of Evangelism and Missions at Southwestern Baptist Theological Seminary, Fort Worth, Texas

"*Evangelism and discipleship are not enemies. They are the best of friends. Two-sides of the same coin. Evangelism invites people into a discipleship journey, and discipleship teaches people to know Jesus and make Him known. I love Pastor Anthony's heart, passion, and practicality for discipleship and evangelism. It shows all through this book. Please, do yourself a favor, and take full advantage of using this material. Your ministry will only benefit from it for the glory of our great God.*"

Shane Pruitt, National Next Gen Evangelism Director – North American Mission Board

"This Bible-based discipleship book is great! It covers the basics very well."

Mike Morris, Director of Applied Ministries, Associate Professor and Bottoms Chair of Missions at Southwestern Baptist Theological Seminary, Fort Worth, Texas

"In a world with so much confusion about the gospel and what many of the primary components of the faith entail, Anthony has put together a helpful tool that churches can use to ensure their people know the foundational truths of following Jesus."

Lance Crowell, Church Ministries Associate of Discipleship Ministries at the Southern Baptist of Texas Convention, Grapevine, Texas

"Dr. Anthony Svajda has given us all a practical tool to fulfill the command to disciple others. While most Christ-followers agree disciple-making and evangelism should be a priority, many struggle to fulfill this command feeling inadequate for the task. But, it is a command nonetheless. Anthony Svajda allows any Christ-follower to begin this God-commanded privilege. With the many other resources available, we are without excuse. "So whoever knows the right thing to do and fails to do it, for him it is sin." (James 4:17, ESV) "Text-Driven Discipleship" provides a simple, yet effective pattern and the necessary connection to local church's role is built in. I am thankful for resources like "Text-Driven Discipleship." Let's pray, read, memorize, attend, and grow together. Let's disciple others."

Wes Hinote, Pastor of Old River Baptist Church, Dayton, Texas

DEDICATION

This discipleship guide is dedicated to every Saint of Jesus Christ, who have been called by their Savior to *"Go and make disciples of all nations"* (Matt 28:18–20).

May this book become a tool for you to raise up a new generation of Christ followers for His church and build your faith as you walk in faithful service to Him.

TABLE OF CONTENTS

INTRODUCTION

Why Another Discipleship Book?

Let's face it. There are a ton of discipleship books out there on the market. Why in all of Christendom do we need another discipleship book?

Let me give you a few reasons why this discipleship book is important and how it is different from any other discipleship book you will get.

1. Discipleship Is Important

When a person reads the New Testament, discipleship is written all over it. Whether Jesus is leading his disciples, Paul is making disciples, or the church is being called to make disciples, discipleship is there. Discipleship in the New Testament is done in a small group or one-on-one, with one believer leading another to know and follow God.

This book is designed to do that. This is not another Bible study or life guide. This is not a preaching series to work through. This book is a guide for one believer to lead another in order to help them know and follow God through studying the text of the Bible.

2. God's Word Is Important

When you look at all the different material labeled as discipleship you can be overrun with options. Some formats are DVD driven, some are book driven, others are conversation driven. But the real basis of teaching people to know and follow God is God's Word.

Therefore, this resource is Text-Driven Discipleship. The guide is designed to help a disciple-maker lead their disciple to discuss and understand God's Word and to help the disciple begin to study God's Word for themselves.

3. God's People Are Important

When Christians look at the church, they should see a group of people committed to making disciples. Making disciples is the Commission of every Christian and the marching orders of the Church (Matt 28:18–20).

Thus, this resource was written in order to help Christians do what they were called to do. This guide is to help God's people teach the Bible to others.

GETTING STARTED

At this point you may be asking yourself, "What did I get myself into?" That is totally normal if you have never gone through discipleship before.

This portion of the book will explain the key elements of a discipleship relationship. As you grow closer to God, this section will help you know what you can expect from discipleship.

If you are the disciple-maker, cover these pillars and the commitment before you work through the rest of the material. You and your disciple must have a clear understanding of what is expected for the relationship to function correctly.

Weekly Discipleship Meetings

Weekly discipleship meetings are a big part of the discipleship process and should be consistent throughout the duration of the material. The bond and the fellowship you will build and share will be life changing. The accountability will help you stick with it. Commit to meeting together each week for this season of discipleship.

At each meeting you should ask your disciple:
- To recite the weekly memory verse.
- To recite the previous weekly memory verses.
- To review their daily devotionals and discuss any questions they may have had.
- To review the previous Sunday's sermon and discuss any questions they may have had.
- To discuss any spiritual issues or questions your disciple may be working through.
- To discuss any new prayer requests or previously mentioned prayer requests.

Daily Bible Studies

Each day there are daily Scripture readings following the weekly sessions. The daily Bible readings provide additional Scripture on the topic discussed during the previous session to help the disciple gain confidence in reading Scripture and form a habit of reading and applying the Bible to your everyday life.

- **Read** - Read the Scripture slowly and think through all that it has to say. Feel free to look it up in your Bible and examine the verses before and after it to get a better understanding.

- **Reflect** - What is the Scripture trying to communicate to you. Is the verse telling you about God? About a fact of life? About a promise of God? About a characteristic of God?

- **Respond** - How does this Scripture apply to you? What is the Word telling you to do?

A Focus on God's Word

The beginning of discipleship starts with the reading and study of God's Word. The Greek word for disciple is Math-et-tes (μαθητης) and means to be a student with an aspect of adhering to what is being learned. In the context of this study, we are students or disciples of God's Word. Therefore, we seek to understand and apply God's Word to our lives.

For more information see "What Is the Bible?" in the appendix.

Weekly Scripture Memory

Scripture memory is a great way to internalize God's Word into your heart and mind. Although some find Scripture memory to be daunting, the practice of working to memorizing the Word of God is greatly beneficial for Christians.

For more information see "Tips for Memorizing Scripture" in the appendix.

Disciple-maker, share some of the benefits you have received from memorizing Scripture with your disciple.

Disciple-maker, share some of your tips to memorize Scripture with your disciple.

Review "Tips for Memorizing Scripture" in the Appendix.

The Discipleship Commitment

Anything worth doing requires a commitment, and the process of discipleship is no different. Over the term of this discipleship relationship you will be challenged and encouraged to go deeper with God than you may have before. The study is designed to stretch you and push you deeper into a relationship with Jesus. If you are ready to go deeper and take the next step, sign and make the commitment for discipleship.

- I commit to be honest and open with my discipleship partner.
- I commit to have an open mind and heart to what the Lord Jesus Christ would show me through his Word and this study.
- I commit to daily read my Bible and record reflections and applications in the daily devotion section of my book.
- I commit to come prepared with my daily devotionals complete and Scriptures memorized to the best of my ability to the weekly discipleship meetings.
- I commit to do my best to memorize the weekly Scripture memory assignments.
- I commit to do my best to attend Sunday services with my local church and take sermon notes in my book to discuss at discipleship meetings.

_____

Disciple

_____

Disciple-Maker

SESSION 1 – WHAT IS THE BIG DEAL ABOUT THE GOSPEL?

Week one is all about the Gospel and what you need to know about it. The Gospel is the starting point for the Christian life. It is the foundation and starting point of walking with Jesus, which must be understood and responded to.

The Greek word for Gospel, e-van-gel-lion (ευαγγελιον) means good news. After studying these passages and understanding what the Gospel is, I truly hope that you find it to be good news as well.

Disciple-maker, have your disciple circle or highlight key phrases of Scripture in their book, and discuss the concepts as found in Scripture with your disciple.

Why Do We Need the Gospel?

"For all have sinned and fall short of the glory of God." (Romans 3:23, CSB)

- According to the Scripture, who has sinned?

- What is sin?

- What are the consequences of sin?

Why do we need the Gospel? Because man has sinned and is separated from God.

Disciple-maker, share some of the ways that you know sin has been or is present in your life with your disciple and ask your disciple how they have sinned.

"For the wages of sin is death, but the gift of God is eternal life in Christ Jesus our Lord." (Romans 6:23, CSB)

- What is a wage?

A wage is something you earn. Just as you earn a day's wage for doing work, because we have broken God's laws by sinning, we have earned punishment for breaking the law.

Why do we need the Gospel? Because man has sinned and is deserving of God's punishment.

God does not punish people unjustly. He simply gives us the consequences of our choices and actions.

- According to the Scripture, what is the wage of sin?

Why do we need the Gospel? Because man has sinned and without God, we deserve spiritual death.

Disciple-maker, discuss the penalty of sin and disobedience to God with your disciple.

What Is the Good News of the Gospel?

"For the wages of sin is death, but the gift of God is eternal life in Christ Jesus our Lord." (Romans 6:23, CSB)

- What is a gift?

A gift is something you cannot earn. Gifts are not given based on a person's ability or achievement, and neither are gifts a payment for doing a job.

What is the good news of the Gospel? God loves us not because we are good, but because He is good.

God does not give us gifts based on who we are. He gives us the gift based on who He is—merciful, gracious, and loving.

- What is the gift that God has given us?

- By whom did that gift come through?

"But God proves his own love for us in that while we were still sinners, Christ died for us." (Romans 5:8, CSB)

- Why did God send Jesus?

- What did God do for sinners through sending Jesus?

> **What is the good news of the Gospel? God loves us, and He sent Jesus to die for us and provide eternal life for those who have faith in Him.**
>
> Disciple-maker, share with your disciple the time you came to know what Jesus had done for you.

Why Should I Receive the Gospel?

"For everyone who calls on the name of the Lord will be saved." (Romans 10:13, CSB)

- Underline the action required to receive salvation.

- Circle the promise given to those who *"call on the name of the Lord."*

- To whom does this verse apply?

- Why is this such good news for those who *"call on the name of the Lord"*?

> **Why should I receive the Gospel? Because if you call upon Jesus for salvation, "you will be saved."**
>
> Disciple-maker, share with your disciple how you have called upon the Lord and continue to call upon Jesus.

"Truly I tell you, anyone who hears my word and believes him who sent me has eternal life and will not come under judgment but has passed from death to life." (John 5:24, CSB)

- Underline the two actions required to receive eternal life.

- Circle the promise given to those *"who hears my word and believes him who sent me."*

- To whom does this verse apply?

- What is so good about the promise of this verse?

> **Why should I receive the Gospel? Because if you call upon Jesus for salvation, you will live with the promise of eternal life.**
>
> Disciple-maker, share with your disciple how the promise of eternal life gives you hope today.

How Do I Receive the Gospel?

"If you confess with your mouth, "Jesus is Lord," and believe in your heart that God raised him from the dead, you will be saved. One believes with the heart, resulting in righteousness, and one confesses with the mouth, resulting in salvation." (Romans 10:9–10, CSB)

- What does it mean to *"confess with your mouth, 'Jesus is Lord'"*?

- What does it imply for your actions to call Jesus your *"Lord"*?

- What does it mean to *"believe in your heart that God raised him from the dead"?*

- What does it imply for your actions to believe that Jesus rose from the dead?

- Circle the promise found in the above Scripture for those who confess with their mouth, *"Jesus is Lord,"* and believe in their heart that *"God raised him from the dead."*

- What results in the life of one who *"believes with the heart"*?

- What results in the life of one who *"confesses with the mouth"*?

"But to all who did receive him, he gave them the right to be children of God, to those who believe in his name." (John 1:12, CSB)

- Underline the two actions described in the passage.

- Circle the promise given to those who believe and receive.

- What does it mean to *"receive him"?*

- What does it mean to *"believe in his name"?*

Are You Ready to Accept the Gospel?

If you are already a believer in Jesus and have received Him as your Lord and Savior, share your testimony of salvation with your disciple-maker.

> Disciple-maker, listen to their testimony and rejoice with your disciple over all God has done.

If you have not made the decision to receive Jesus as your Lord and Savior, talk with your disciple-maker about how to proceed.

Disciple-maker, this is your time to ask the disciple to make a decision for Jesus.

Begin by asking your disciple if they are ready to begin a relationship with Jesus.

Before the disciple makes a commitment for Christ, the disciple-maker must make sure they understand the commitment they are making.

Confirm their understanding by asking the following questions.

What is sin?

How have you sinned?

What is the effect of sin on man's relationship with God?

What is the punishment for sin?

What did God do for sinners through Jesus?

From this momen will you follow Jesus?

Will you do what He calls you to do no matter the costs?

If they cannot verbalize the answer to these questions, spend some time discussing them until your disciple understands.

If your disciple is able to answer these questions with confidence, ask them to call out to God for salvation.

Jesus, I am a sinner. I have sinned by_____.
I believe that you are God and Savoir.
Thank you for dying on the cross for my sins and giving me eternal life.
From this point on, I will follow you no matter the costs.
I am yours and You are my Lord.
Amen.

When your disciple prays for salvation, encourage them and rejoice with them!

Week 1 Day 1 – WHAT IS THE BIG DEAL ABOUT THE GOSPEL?

Weekly Scripture Memory:
    Romans 6:23
    2 Corinthians 5:17

Read - Romans 6:23
"For the wages of sin is death, but the gift of God is eternal life in Christ Jesus our Lord." (Romans 6:23, CSB)

Reflect - What does this verse tell you...
about God?

_____

_____

about yourself?

_____

_____

about God's grace?

_____

_____

Respond - Is there something that you need to...
know about?

_____

_____

share or do?

_____

_____

praise God for?

_____

_____

pray over?

_____

_____

Week 1 Day 2 – WHAT IS THE BIG DEAL ABOUT THE GOSPEL?

Weekly Scripture Memory:
>Romans 6:23
>2 Corinthians 5:17

Read - 2 Corinthians 5:17

"Therefore, if anyone is in Christ, he is a new creation; the old has passed away, and see, the new has come!" (2 Corinthians 5:17, CSB)

Reflect - What does this verse tell you…

about God?

----

about yourself?

----

about God's grace?

Respond - Is there something that you need to…

know about?

----

share or do?

----

praise God for?

----

pray over?

Week 1 Day 3 – WHAT IS THE BIG DEAL ABOUT THE GOSPEL?

Write - Romans 6:23

_____

_____

Write - 2 Corinthians 5:17

_____

_____

Read - John 3:16
"For God loved the world in this way: He gave his one and only Son, so that everyone who believes in him will not perish but have eternal life." (John 3:16, CSB)

Reflect - What does this verse tell you...
about God?

_____

_____

about yourself?

_____

_____

about God's grace?

_____

_____

Respond - Is there something that you need to...
know about?

_____

share or do?

_____

praise God for?

_____

pray over?

_____

Week 1 Day 4 – WHAT IS THE BIG DEAL ABOUT THE GOSPEL?

Write - Romans 6:23

Write - 2 Corinthians 5:17

Read - 2 Corinthians 5:21
"He made the one who did not know sin to be sin for us, so that in him we might become the righteousness of God." (2 Corinthians 5:21, CSB)

Reflect - What does this verse tell you...
about God?

----

about yourself?

----

about God's grace?

Respond - Is there something that you need to...
know about?
----

share or do?
----

praise God for?
----

pray over?

Week 1 Day 5 – WHAT IS THE BIG DEAL ABOUT THE GOSPEL?

Write - Romans 6:23

Write - 2 Corinthians 5:17

Read - Ephesians 2:1–10

"And you were dead in your trespasses and sins in which you previously lived according to the ways of this world, according to the ruler of the power of the air, the spirit now working in the disobedient. We too all previously lived among them in our fleshly desires, carrying out the inclinations of our flesh and thoughts, and we were by nature children under wrath as the others were also. But God, who is rich in mercy, because of his great love that he had for us, made us alive with Christ even though we were dead in trespasses. You are saved by grace! He also raised us up with him and seated us with him in the heavens in Christ Jesus, so that in the coming ages he might display the immeasurable riches of his grace through his kindness to us in Christ Jesus. For you are saved by grace through faith, and this is not from yourselves; it is God's gift—not from works, so that no one can boast. For we are his workmanship, created in Christ Jesus for good works, which God prepared ahead of time for us to do." (Ephesians 2:1–10, CSB)

Reflect - What does this verse tell you…

about God?

----

about yourself?

----

about God's grace?

Respond - Is there something that you need to...
know about?

----

share or do?

----

praise God for?

----

pray over?

Week 1 Day 6 – WHAT IS THE BIG DEAL
ABOUT THE GOSPEL?

Write - Romans 6:23

Write - 2 Corinthians 5:17

Read- 1 John 1:9
*"If we confess our sins, he is faithful and righteous to forgive us
our sins and to cleanse us from all unrighteousness."* (1 John 1:9,
CSB)

Reflect - What does this verse tell you…
about God?

---

about yourself?

---

about God's grace?

Respond - Is there something that you need to…
know about?

---

share or do?

---

praise God for?

---

pray over?

Week 1 Day 7 – WHAT IS THE BIG DEAL ABOUT THE GOSPEL?

Write - Romans 6:23

Write - 2 Corinthians 5:17

Sermon Notes

Speaker:

Date:

Text:

SESSION 2 – WHAT DOES IT MEAN TO BE SAVED?

Week two is about what it means to have experienced salvation. Those who have confessed that "Christ is Lord," and believe that God raised him from the dead can be confident that their sins have been forgiven and that they have a relationship with God (Romans 10:9).

According to the Bible, at salvation believers receive a new identity, are adopted, are redeemed, are given an inheritance, and are assured that they will never be forsaken. They are now "in Christ."

> Disciple-maker,
> 1) Review the Scripture memory from the previous week.
> 2) Review last week's daily devotionals and sermon notes.
> 3) Pray over the meeting with your disciple before starting.
> 4) Have your disciples circle or highlight key phrases of the Scriptures in their book and discuss the concepts as found in the Scriptures with your disciple.

What Does It Mean to be Saved?

"Paul, an apostle of Christ Jesus by God's will:
To the faithful saints in Christ Jesus at Ephesus.
Grace to you and peace from God our Father and the Lord Jesus Christ." (Ephesians 1:1–2, CSB)

- What do you think Paul is communicating by referring to "the faithful saints"?

- Underline the next words in the passage that explains the relationship that determines this new identity.

- Why do you think Paul calls God "our Father"?

Paul writes to "the faithful saints," or hagiois (ἁγίοις), literally, "holy ones." But that new identity—saints—is reliant upon a relationship.

What does it mean to be saved? We have a new identity and relationship with God. We are "in Christ."

What Does It Mean to Be Saved?

"Blessed is the God and Father of our Lord Jesus Christ, who has blessed us with every spiritual blessing in the heavens in Christ. For he chose us in him, before the foundation of the world, to be holy and blameless in love before him. He predestined us to be adopted as sons through Jesus Christ for himself, according to the good pleasure of his will, to the praise of his glorious grace that he lavished on us in the Beloved One." (Ephesians 1:3–6, CSB)

- What do you think it means that God "has blessed us with every spiritual blessing in the heavens"?

- Underline the two words at the end of verse 3 that speak to where those blessings exist.

- What do you think it means that those blessings are "in Christ"?

What does it mean to be saved? We have been adopted into the family of God.

We have received a special relationship with Christ. There is nothing more important.

- What do you think is the purpose of our salvation, according to this passage?

- What does it mean that "he chose us" and "He predestined us"?

> Prevent your disciple from chasing the doctrine of predestination for too long. While this doctrine is important, this is not the main question we are seeking to answer. The emphasis here is not *when* God did it, but that *He did it* and *we did not!*

- What does it mean to be "adopted as sons"?

- Paul says that God lavished grace upon us, and that grace comes (no doubt you're sensing a pattern here) "in the Beloved One." Underline that phrase.

> Our salvation is a gift of God. Christians are those who have been set apart by God to be adopted as sons. But that adoption comes by way of that special relationship.
>
> Emphasize that relationship. Have your disciple underline those two words: "through Christ."

What Does It Mean to Be Saved?.

"In him we have redemption through his blood, the forgiveness of our trespasses, according to the riches of his grace that he richly poured out on us with all wisdom and understanding. He made known to us the mystery of his will, according to his good pleasure that he purposed in Christ as a plan for the right time— to bring everything together in Christ, both things in heaven and things on earth in him." (Ephesians 1:7–10, CSB)

- What does it mean that "we have redemption through his blood"?

- What is redemption?

- Underline each occurrence of "in him" and "in Christ" in this passage. What does this remind us concerning all of these blessings?

This is a good time to remind your disciple of the wages of sin (Romans 6:23), the necessity of the shedding of blood for the forgiveness of sins (Hebrews 9:22), and the precious blood of Christ shed for us (1 Peter 1:18–19).

Redemption means that we our salvation came at a cost—the shed blood of Jesus.

What does it mean to be saved? We have been redeemed through Jesus' sacrifice.

What Does It Mean to Be Saved?

"In him we have also received an inheritance, because we were predestined according to the plan of the one who works out everything in agreement with the purpose of his will, so that we who had already put our hope in Christ might bring praise to his glory." (Ephesians 1:11–12, CSB)

- Underline the phrase "In him" in verse 11 and "in Christ" in verse 12. What is significant about those phrases in this passage?

- What does it mean to receive an inheritance? How is this connected to verse 5?

- According to this passage, what is the proper response to the realization that God's good plans for his people will be fulfilled?

What does it mean to be saved? We have been given an inheritance.

Our receiving an inheritance is due to our having been "adopted as sons" (v. 5).

What Does It Mean to Be Saved?

"In him you also—when you heard the word of truth, the gospel of your salvation, and when you also believed—were sealed in him with the promise of the Holy Spirit. He is the down payment of our inheritance, until the redemption of the possession, to the praise of his glory." (Ephesians 1:13–14, CSB)

- Underline the two instances of "in him."

- What is the promise of the Holy Spirit?

- At what point were you sealed and given the Holy Spirit?

- What does a down payment signify?

What does it mean to be saved? We are secure in our salvation.

Once a person is saved, they are sealed and secured by the Holy Spirit as a promise of eternal life.

Do You Understand What It Means to Be Saved?

Spend a few minutes talking about salvation with your discipleship partner. Rejoice in what God has done for you and pray together thanking God for salvation through Jesus Christ.

Week 2 Day 1 – WHAT DOES IT MEAN TO BE SAVED?

Review:
> Romans 6:23
> 2 Corinthians 5:17

Read - Ephesians 1:7
"In him we have redemption through his blood, the forgiveness of our trespasses, according to the riches of his grace." (Ephesians 1:7, CSB)

Reflect - What does this verse tell you...
about God?

----

about yourself?

----

about God's plan?

Respond - Is there something that you need to...
know about?

----

share or do?

----

praise God for?

----

pray over?

Week 2 Day 2 – WHAT DOES IT MEAN TO BE SAVED?

Review:
>   Romans 6:23
>   2 Corinthians 5:17

Write - Ephesians 1:7

Read - Galatians 4:4–5

"When the time came to completion, God sent his Son, born of a woman, born under law, to redeem those under the law, so that we might receive adoption as sons." (Galatians 4:4–5, CSB)

Reflect - What does this verse tell you...

about God?

----

about yourself?

----

about God's plan?

Respond - Is there something that you need to...

know about?

----

share or do?

----

praise God for?

----

pray over?

Week 2 Day 3 – WHAT DOES IT MEAN TO BE SAVED?

Review:
        Romans 6:23
        2 Corinthians 5:17

Write - Ephesians 1:7

Write - Galatians 4:4–5

Read - Romans 3:24
"They are justified freely by his grace through the redemption that is in Christ Jesus." (Romans 3:24, CSB)

Reflect - What does this verse tell you...
about God?

----

about yourself?

----

about God's grace?

Respond - Is there something that you need to...

know about?

_____

_____

_____

share or do?

_____

_____

_____

praise God for?

_____

_____

_____

pray over?

_____

_____

_____

Week 2 Day 4 – WHAT DOES IT MEAN TO BE SAVED?

Review:
> Romans 6:23
> 2 Corinthians 5:17

Write - Ephesians 1:7

Write - Galatians 4:4–5

Read - Romans 5:1

"Since we have been declared righteous by faith, we have peace with God through our Lord Jesus Christ." (Romans 5:1, CSB)

Reflect - What does this verse tell you...

about God?

----

about yourself?

----

about God's grace?

Respond - Is there something that you need to...

know about?

_____

_____

share or do?

_____

_____

praise God for?

_____

_____

pray over?

_____

_____

Week 2 Day 5 – WHAT DOES IT MEAN TO BE SAVED?

Review:
      Romans 6:23
      2 Corinthians 5:17

Write - Ephesians 1:7

Write - Galatians 4:4–5

Read - Colossians 3:3–4

"For you died, and your life is hidden with Christ in God. When Christ, who is your life, appears, then you also will appear with him in glory." (Colossians 3:3–4, CSB)

Reflect - What does this verse tell you...
about God?

----

about yourself?

----

about God's grace?

Respond - Is there something that you need to...

know about?

_____

_____

share or do?

_____

_____

praise God for?

_____

_____

pray over?

_____

_____

_____

Week 2 Day 6 – WHAT DOES IT MEAN TO BE SAVED?

Review:
>   Romans 6:23
>   2 Corinthians 5:17

Write - Ephesians 1:7

Write - Galatians 4:4–5

Read - 1 Peter 1:3–4

"Blessed be the God and Father of our Lord Jesus Christ. Because of his great mercy he has given us new birth into a living hope through the resurrection of Jesus Christ from the dead and into an inheritance that is imperishable, undefiled, and unfading, kept in heaven for you." (1 Peter 1:3–4, CSB)

Reflect - What does this verse tell you...

about God?

----

about yourself?

----

about God's grace?

Respond - Is there something that you need to...

know about?

share or do?

praise God for?

pray over?

Week 2 Day 7– WHAT DOES IT MEAN TO BE SAVED?

Review:
    Romans 6:23
    2 Corinthians 5:17

Write - Ephesians 1:7

Write - Galatians 4:4–5

Sermon Notes

Speaker:

Date:

Text:

SESSION 3 – WHAT IS THE BIG DEAL ABOUT BAPTISM?

Week three is about baptism and what you need to know about it. Baptism is the first act of obedience in the Christian life. It is the first act of a Christian to witness of their new life walking with Jesus.

Disciple-maker,
1) Review the Scripture memory from week one.
2) Review last week's daily devotionals and sermon notes.
3) Pray over the meeting with your disciple before starting.
4) Have your disciples circle or highlight key phrases of the Scriptures In their book and discuss the concepts as found in the Scriptures with your disciple.

Who Should Be Baptized?

Peter replied, "Repent and be baptized, each of you, in the name of Jesus Christ for the forgiveness of your sins, and you will receive the gift of the Holy Spirit. For the promise is for you and for your children, and for all who are far off, as many as the Lord our God will call." With many other words he testified and strongly urged them, saying, "Be saved from this corrupt generation!" So those who accepted his message were baptized, and that day about three thousand people were added to them. (Acts 2:38–41, CSB)

- After Peter preached at Pentecost, the people who heard the message needed a way to respond. Circle the instruction that Peter gave to those who needed to respond.

- Repentance is the first instruction given for salvation, and then baptism was to follow. What does this tell you about who should be baptized?

> **Who should be baptized? Those who have repented from sin and turned their lives over to Jesus.**
>
> For the person who was baptized, baptism was the first step of obedience after receiving salvation through Jesus Christ.

- Look back to the last sentence of Acts 2:38–41. The Scripture says, *"So those who accepted his message were baptized, and that day about three thousand people were added to them."* What was the church's action after the new believer was baptized?

> **Who should be baptized? Those who want to share their new relationship with Jesus.**
>
> Baptism was the moment for the new believers to stand up before their church family and say, "I am now walking with Jesus." For the church, baptism was a way to observe the decision of the new believer and accept them into their fellowship.

What Does Baptism Communicate?

*"Therefore we were **buried** with him by baptism into **death**, in order that, just as Christ was **raised** from the **dead** by the glory of the Father, so we too may walk in **newness** of life. For if we have been united with him in the likeness of his **death**, we will certainly also be in the likeness of his **resurrection**. For we know that our old self was **crucified** with him so that the body ruled by sin might be rendered powerless so that we may no longer be enslaved to sin, since a person who has **died** is freed from sin. Now if we **died** with Christ, we believe that we will also live with him, because we know that Christ, having been **raised** from the dead, will not die again. **Death** no longer rules over him. For the **death** he died, he **died** to sin once for all time; but the life he **lives**, he **lives** to God. So, you too consider yourselves **dead** to sin and **alive** to God in Christ Jesus."* (Romans 6:4–11, CSB)

- This passage uses the symbolism of baptism to illustrate the death of the old life and the resurrection to new life as found in Christ. In the above Scripture underline the words that indicate "Death" and "Resurrection" in **bold**.

- The passage is aligning the death and resurrection of Christ with the death of the old life and new life found in Jesus for the believer. In the above Scripture, circle the references to Jesus and you.

- What does this tell us about the symbolism and method of baptism?

What does baptism communicate? What Jesus has done for us.

When a person is baptized by immersion, they are illustrating what Jesus Christ has done for them. Just as Christ died on the cross and was buried, we are put under the surface of the water symbolizing death to our old lives of sin. On the third day Christ rose from death, and we too rise from the water symbolizing our new lives walking with Jesus.

Fun fact: even the Greek term for baptism, Bap-Tyz-O (βαπτιζο) illustrates this truth as well. βαπτιζο literally means 'to immerse or plunge in water.'
The Greek terminology tells us how to practice the ordinance of baptism by immersion because just as we are buried (immersed) with Christ, we are raised again to newness of life in Jesus.

- What good news does this passage tell those who have trusted in Christ? Cross Reference 2 Corinthians 5:17.

> "Therefore, if anyone is in Christ, he is a new creation; the old has passed away, and see, the new has come!" (2 Corinthians 5:17, CSB)
>
> **What does baptism communicate? Christians are made a new creation in Christ.**
>
> Baptism demonstrates that for those in Christ, the old life is gone and they are now living a new life with Jesus.

- What does this passage tell us about the new life of those who have trusted in Christ? Cross reference Galatians 2:20.

> "I have been crucified with Christ, and I no longer live, but Christ lives in me. The life I now live in the body, I live by faith in the Son of God, who loved me and gave himself for me." (Galatians 2:20, CSB)
>
> **What does baptism communicate? We have died to our old lives.**
>
> Baptism demonstrates that our old lives have been put to death and we are now living lives following Jesus.

What Does Baptism Do?

"For we were all baptized by one Spirit into one body—whether Jews or Greeks, whether slaves or free—and we were all given one Spirit to drink." (1 Corinthians 12:13, CSB)

- According to this Scripture what does the act of baptism add the believer to?

What does baptism do? Baptism unifies a believer to the Church

Baptism is the believer's opportunity to witness before others what Christ has done for them and declare that they are now unified with other Christ followers. Baptism also allows other Christ followers to identify the new believers among them and accept them into the family.

Are You Ready to Be Baptized?

If you have been baptized, share your story of baptism with your discipleship partner.

Disciple-maker, listen to their testimony and rejoice with your disciple over all God has done.

If you have not been baptized, discuss any questions you have about baptism with your discipleship partner and pray through any obstacle that would keep you from being baptized.

Disciple-maker, discuss and answer their questions. Encourage your disciple to be baptized and connect your disciple with your pastor in order to make arrangements for baptism.

Week 3 Day 1 – WHAT IS THE BIG DEAL ABOUT BAPTISM?

Review:
Romans 6:23
2 Corinthians 5:17
Ephesians 1:7
Galatians 4:4–5

Read - 1 Corinthians 12:13
"For we were all baptized by one Spirit into one body—whether Jews or Greeks, whether slaves or free—and we were all given one Spirit to drink." (1 Corinthians 12:13, CSB)

Reflect - What does this verse tell you...
about God?

----

about yourself?

----

about God's grace?

Respond - Is there something that you need to...
know about?

----

share or do?

----

praise God for?

----

pray over?

Week 3 Day 2 – WHAT IS THE BIG DEAL ABOUT BAPTISM?

Review:
Romans 6:23
2 Corinthians 5:17
Ephesians 1:7
Galatians 4:4–5

Write - 1 Corinthians 12:13

Read - Matthew 3:13–17
"Then Jesus came from Galilee to John at the Jordan, to be baptized by him. But John tried to stop him, saying, 'I need to be baptized by you, and yet you come to me?' Jesus answered him, 'Allow it for now, because this is the way for us to fulfill all righteousness.' Then John allowed him to be baptized. When Jesus was baptized, he went up immediately from the water. The heavens suddenly opened for him, and he saw the Spirit of God descending like a dove and coming down on him. And a voice from heaven said: 'This is my beloved Son, with whom I am well-pleased.'" (Matthew 3:13–17, CSB)

Reflect - What does this verse tell you...
about God?

----

about yourself?

----

about God's grace?

Respond - Is there something that you need to...

know about?

_____

_____

_____

share or do?

_____

_____

praise God for?

_____

_____

pray over?

_____

_____

Week 3 Day 3 – WHAT IS THE BIG DEAL ABOUT BAPTISM?

Review:
> Romans 6:23
> 2 Corinthians 5:17
> Ephesians 1:7
> Galatians 4:4–5

Write - 1 Corinthians 12:13

Read - Galatians 3:23–29

"Before this faith came, we were confined under the law, imprisoned until the coming faith was revealed. The law, then, was our guardian until Christ, so that we could be justified by faith. But since that faith has come, we are no longer under a guardian, for through faith you are all sons of God in Christ Jesus. For those of you who were baptized into Christ have been clothed with Christ. There is no Jew or Greek, slave or free, male and female; since you are all one in Christ Jesus. And if you belong to Christ, then you are Abraham's seed, heirs according to the promise." (Galatians 3:23–29, CSB)

Reflect - What does this verse tell you...
about God?

----

about yourself?

----

about God's grace?

Respond - Is there something that you need to...
know about?

----

share or do?

----

praise God for?

----

pray over?

Week 3 Day 4 – WHAT IS THE BIG DEAL ABOUT BAPTISM?

Review:
> Romans 6:23
> 2 Corinthians 5:17
> Ephesians 1:7
> Galatians 4:4–5

Write - 1 Corinthians 12:13

Read -Colossians 2:10–14

"and you have been filled by him, who is the head over every ruler and authority. You were also circumcised in him with a circumcision not done with hands, by putting off the body of flesh, in the circumcision of Christ, when you were buried with him in baptism, in which you were also raised with him through faith in the working of God, who raised him from the dead. And when you were dead in trespasses and in the uncircumcision of your flesh, he made you alive with him and forgave us all our trespasses. He erased the certificate of debt, with its obligations, that was against us and opposed to us, and has taken it away by nailing it to the cross." (Colossians 2:10–14, CSB)

Reflect - What does this verse tell you...

about God?

----

about yourself?

----

about God's grace?

Respond - Is there something that you need to...
know about?

----

share or do?

----

praise God for?

----

pray over?

Week 3 Day 5 – WHAT IS THE BIG DEAL ABOUT BAPTISM?

Review:
Romans 6:23
2 Corinthians 5:17
Ephesians 1:7
Galatians 4:4–5

Write - 1 Corinthians 12:13

Read - 1 Peter 3:18–22
"For Christ also suffered for sins once for all, the righteous for the unrighteous, that he might bring you to God. He was put to death in the flesh but made alive by the Spirit, in which he also went and made proclamation to the spirits in prison who in the past were disobedient, when God patiently waited in the days of Noah while the ark was being prepared. In it a few—that is, eight people—were saved through water. Baptism, which corresponds to this, now saves you (not as the removal of dirt from the body, but the pledge of a good conscience toward God) through the resurrection of Jesus Christ, who has gone into heaven and is at the right hand of God with angels, authorities, and powers subject to him." (1 Peter 3:18–22, CSB)

Reflect - What does this verse tell you...
about God?

----

about yourself?

----

about God's grace?

Respond - Is there something that you need to...

know about?

share or do?

praise God for?

pray over?

Week 3 Day 6 – WHAT IS THE BIG DEAL ABOUT BAPTISM?

Review:

Romans 6:23
2 Corinthians 5:17
Ephesians 1:7
Galatians 4:4–5

Write - 1 Corinthians 12:13

- -

- -

Read- John 3:3–8

"Jesus replied, 'Truly I tell you, unless someone is born again, he cannot see the kingdom of God.' 'How can anyone be born when he is old?' Nicodemus asked him. 'Can he enter his mother's womb a second time and be born?' Jesus answered, 'Truly I tell you, unless someone is born of water and the Spirit, he cannot enter the kingdom of God. Whatever is born of the flesh is flesh, and whatever is born of the Spirit is spirit. Do not be amazed that I told you that you must be born again. The wind blows where it pleases, and you hear its sound, but you don't know where it comes from or where it is going. So it is with everyone born of the Spirit.'" (John 3:3–8, CSB)

Reflect - What does this verse tell you...

about God?

- -

- -

about yourself?

- -

- -

about God's grace?

- -

- -

Respond - Is there something that you need to...
know about?

share or do?

praise God for?

pray over?

Week 3 Day 7 – WHAT IS THE BIG DEAL ABOUT BAPTISM?

Review:
    Romans 6:23
    2 Corinthians 5:17
    Ephesians 1:7
    Galatians 4:4–5

Write - 1 Corinthians 12:13

Sermon Notes
Speaker:

Date:

Text:

SESSION 4 – WHAT IS THE BIG DEAL ABOUT CHURCH?

Week four is all about the basics of the local church. The local church is referred to as the Body of Christ. The symbol of Christ's body represents how all believers are unified together in belief, practice, and mission for Christ.

The Greek word for church, ek-a-la-see-ah (ἐκκλησία) means the called-out ones who are gathered together. After studying the church through God's Word this week, I hope you will see the necessity of gathering and worshiping together with other Christians.

Disciple-maker,
1) Review the Scripture memory from the previous weeks.
2) Review last week's daily devotionals and sermon notes.
3) Pray over the meeting with your disciple before starting.
4) Have your disciples circle or highlight key phrases of the Scriptures in their book and discuss the concepts as found in the Scriptures with your disciple.

What Is the Church?

"Simon Peter answered, 'You are the Messiah, the Son of the living God.' Jesus responded, 'Blessed are you, Simon son of Jonah, because flesh and blood did not reveal this to you, but my Father in heaven. And I also say to you that you are Peter, and on this rock I will build my church, and the gates of Hades will not overpower it." (Matthew 16:16–18, CSB)

- What is the *"rock"* on which Jesus will build his church?

- What does the foundation tell us about the church?

What is the Church? A gathering of believers

Make sure to emphasize Peter's faith and confession in Jesus is the foundation of the church. Lead the disciple to understand that a church must be made up of believers who confess Jesus.

"So those who accepted his message were baptized, and that day about three thousand people were added to them. They devoted themselves to the apostles' teaching, to the fellowship, to the breaking of bread, and to prayer." (Acts 2:41–42, CSB)

- Who are those that were baptized?

- What are the two qualifications to join a church according to this passage?

- What are the responsibilities of a church member in this passage?

What is the Church? A gathering of devoted believers

The church is a local gathering of baptized believers who see themselves as responsible for one another physically and spiritually. In this way we can speak of the local church as our family. In this passage it is important to note that a church devotes themselves to the teaching of the apostles, the Lord's supper, prayer, and care for one another.

"Let us hold on to the confession of our hope without wavering, since he who promised is faithful. And let us watch out for one another to provoke love and good works, not neglecting to gather together, as some are in the habit of doing, but encouraging each other, and all the more as you see the day approaching." (Hebrews 10:23–25, CSB)

- What does the author of Hebrews say we ought to hold onto?

- According to this passage, what does a church member do?

What is the Church? A gathering of encouraging believers

A local church is a gathering of Christians who collectively affirm one another and encourage one another in their walk with Jesus.

"Peter replied, 'Repent and be baptized, each of you, in the name of Jesus Christ for the forgiveness of your sins, and you will receive the gift of the Holy Spirit.'" (Acts 2:37, CSB)

"In the same way the Spirit also helps us in our weakness, because we do not know what to pray for as we should, but the Spirit himself intercedes for us with unspoken groanings. And he who searches our hearts knows the mind of the Spirit, because he intercedes for the saints according to the will of God." (Romans 8:26–27, CSB)

- Who receives the Holy Spirit in Acts 2?

- What unifies the church together in Romans 8?

- What is the power behind prayer?

What is the Church? A gathering of Spirit-filled believers

Our unity in the churches is based upon the divine fellowship given by the Holy Spirit. Therefore, church membership is bonded by the Holy Spirit's fellowship and church gatherings are aided by the presence of the Holy Spirit.

Why Join a Local Church?

"But you are a chosen race, a royal priesthood, a holy people for his possession, so that you may proclaim the praises of the one who called you out of darkness into his marvelous light. Once you were not a people, but now you are God's people; you had not received mercy, but now you have received mercy." (1 Peter 2:9–10, CSB)

- Is sanctification individual or corporate in this passage? Can one be a healthy Christian without becoming a part of the local church?
- Does the identity of a Christian in this passage allow for one to not be a part of the church?

Why join a local church? Because God has made you a part of his people.

Committing to the local church is the natural outcome of being a Christian. Commitment to the church tells Christians and the community that you have committed your life to Christ and shares what Christ has done for you

If a person is unwilling to connect to the family of God, their actions lead others to wonder if they are connected to God at all.

"So if one member suffers, all the members suffer with it; if one member is honored, all the members rejoice with it. Now you are the body of Christ, and individual members of it. And God has appointed these in the church: first apostles, second prophets, third teachers, next miracles, then gifts of healing, helping, administrating, various kinds of tongues." (1 Corinthians 12:26–28, CSB)

- How should a church member think about other church members?

- Does any church member lack a place to serve in the church?

Why join a local church? To be a part of a team to reach the lost.

Encourage your disciple to find a place to serve in their church. Remind them the Holy Spirit dwelling within them has given them a special place and gifting to serve.

Are You Read to Join the Local Church?

If you are already a member of a local church, discuss with your discipleship partner about your involvement there and also discuss how you can be better involved with your church from what you have learned in this session.

If you are not a member of a local church, tell your discipleship partner why and discuss any questions you have about becoming a church member.

Disciple-maker, share your experience as a church member with your disciple and encourage them to become a faithful church member.

Week 4 Day 1 – WHAT IS THE BIG DEAL ABOUT CHURCH?

Review:
    Romans 6:23
    2 Corinthians 5:17
    Ephesians 1:7
    Galatians 4:4–5
    1 Corinthians 12:13

Read - John 13:34–35

"I give you a new command: Love one another. Just as I have loved you, you are also to love one another. By this everyone will know that you are my disciples, if you love one another." (John 13:34–35, CSB)

Reflect - What does this verse tell you...

about God?

----

about yourself?

----

about God's plan?

Respond - Is there something that you need to...

know about?

----

share or do?

----

praise God for?

----

pray over?

Week 4 Day 2 – WHAT IS THE BIG DEAL ABOUT CHURCH?

Review:

> Romans 6:23
> 2 Corinthians 5:17
> Ephesians 1:7
> Galatians 4:4–5
> 1 Corinthians 12:13

Write - John 13:34–35

Read - Hebrews 10:24–25

"And let us watch out for one another to provoke love and good works, not neglecting to gather together, as some are in the habit of doing, but encouraging each other, and all the more as you see the day approaching." (Hebrews 10:24–25, CSB)

Reflect - What does this verse tell you...

about God?

----

about yourself?

----

about God's plan?

Respond - Is there something that you need to...

know about?

----

share or do?

----

praise God for?

----

pray over?

Week 4 Day 3 – WHAT IS THE BIG DEAL ABOUT CHURCH?

Review:
  Romans 6:23
  2 Corinthians 5:17
  Ephesians 1:7
  Galatians 4:4–5
  1 Corinthians 12:13

Write - John 13:34–35

Write - Hebrews 10:24–25

Read - John 16:5–15

"But now I am going away to him who sent me, and not one of you asks me, 'Where are you going?' Yet, because I have spoken these things to you, sorrow has filled your heart. Nevertheless, I am telling you the truth. It is for your benefit that I go away, because if I don't go away the Counselor will not come to you. If I go, I will send him to you. When he comes, he will convict the world about sin, righteousness, and judgment: About sin, because they do not believe in me; about righteousness, because I am going to the Father and you will no longer see me; and about judgment, because the ruler of this world has been judged. "I still have many things to tell you, but you can't bear them now. When the Spirit of truth comes, he will guide you into all the truth. For he will not speak on his own, but he will speak whatever he hears. He will also declare to you what is to come. He will glorify me, because he will take from what is mine and declare it to you. Everything the Father has is mine. This is why I told you that he takes from what is mine and will declare it to you." (John 16:5–15, CSB)

Reflect - What does this verse tell you...

about God?

----

about yourself?

----

about God's grace?

Respond - Is there something that you need to...

know about?

----

share or do?

----

praise God for?

----

pray over?

Week 4 Day 4 – WHAT IS THE BIG DEAL ABOUT CHURCH?

Review:
>Romans 6:23
>2 Corinthians 5:17
>Ephesians 1:7
>Galatians 4:4–5
>1 Corinthians 12:13

Write - John 13:34–35

Write - Hebrews 10:24–25

Read -Romans 15:1–6

"Now we who are strong have an obligation to bear the weaknesses of those without strength, and not to please ourselves. Each one of us is to please his neighbor for his good, to build him up. For even Christ did not please himself. On the contrary, as it is written, The insults of those who insult you have fallen on me. For whatever was written in the past was written for our instruction, so that we may have hope through endurance and through the encouragement from the Scriptures. Now may the God who gives endurance and encouragement grant you to live in harmony with one another, according to Christ Jesus, so that you may glorify the God and Father of our Lord Jesus Christ with one mind and one voice." (Romans 15:1–6, CSB)

Reflect - What does this verse tell you...

about God?

_____

_____

_____

about yourself?

_____

_____

_____

about God's grace?

_____

_____

Respond - Is there something that you need to...

know about?

_____

_____

_____

share or do?

_____

_____

_____

praise God for?

_____

_____

_____

pray over?

_____

_____

_____

Week 4 Day 5 – WHAT IS THE BIG DEAL ABOUT CHURCH?

Review:

> Romans 6:23
> 2 Corinthians 5:17
> Ephesians 1:7
> Galatians 4:4–5
> 1 Corinthians 12:13

Write - John 13:34–35

Write - Hebrews 10:24–25

Read - 1 Corinthians 12:25–31

"so that there would be no division in the body, but that the members would have the same concern for each other. So if one member suffers, all the members suffer with it; if one member is honored, all the members rejoice with it. Now you are the body of Christ, and individual members of it. And God has appointed these in the church: first apostles, second prophets, third teachers, next miracles, then gifts of healing, helping, administrating, various kinds of tongues. Are all apostles? Are all prophets? Are all teachers? Do all do miracles? Do all have gifts of healing? Do all speak in other tongues? Do all interpret? But desire the greater gifts. And I will show you an even better way."
(1 Corinthians 12:25–31, CSB)

Reflect - What does this verse tell you...

about God?

----

about yourself?

----

about God's grace?

Respond - Is there something that you need to...

know about?

----

share or do?

----

praise God for?

----

pray over?

Week 4 Day 6 – WHAT IS THE BIG DEAL ABOUT CHURCH?

Review:
Romans 6:23
2 Corinthians 5:17
Ephesians 1:7
Galatians 4:4–5
1 Corinthians 12:13

Write - John 13:34–35

Write - Hebrews 10:24–25

Read- Ephesians 4:25–5:2

"Therefore, putting away lying, speak the truth, each one to his neighbor, because we are members of one another. Be angry and do not sin. Don't let the sun go down on your anger, and don't give the devil an opportunity. Let the thief no longer steal. Instead, he is to do honest work with his own hands, so that he has something to share with anyone in need. No foul language should come from your mouth, but only what is good for building up someone in need, so that it gives grace to those who hear. And don't grieve God's Holy Spirit. You were sealed by him for the day of redemption. Let all bitterness, anger and wrath, shouting and slander be removed from you, along with all malice. And be kind and compassionate to one another, forgiving one another, just as God also forgave you in Christ. Therefore, be imitators of God, as dearly loved children, and walk in love, as Christ also loved us and gave himself for us, a sacrificial and fragrant offering to God." (Ephesians 4:25–5:2, CSB)

Reflect - What does this verse tell you…

about God?

----

about yourself?

----

about God's grace?

Respond - Is there something that you need to…

know about?

----

share or do?

----

praise God for?

----

pray over?

Week 4 Day 7– WHAT IS THE BIG DEAL ABOUT CHURCH?

Review:
> Romans 6:23
> 2 Corinthians 5:17
> Ephesians 1:7
> Galatians 4:4–5
> 1 Corinthians 12:13

Write - John 13:34–35

Write - Hebrews 10:24–25

Sermon Notes

Speaker:

Date:

Text:

SESSION 5 – WHAT IS THE BIG DEAL ABOUT DISCIPLESHIP?

Week five is all about discipleship. Although you have now experienced four weeks of discipleship and may be familiar with how it works, this session will be dedicated to defining discipleship according to the Scripture and understanding why discipleship is so important to the Christian life.

Disciple-maker,
1) Review the Scripture memory from the previous weeks.
2) Review last week's daily devotionals and sermon notes.
3) Pray over the meeting with your disciple before starting.
4) Have your disciples circle or highlight key phrases of the Scriptures in their book and discuss the concepts as found in the Scriptures with your disciple.

Why Do Christians Make Disciples?

"Jesus came near and said to them, 'All authority has been given to me in heaven and on earth. Go, therefore, and make disciples of all nations, baptizing them in the name of the Father and of the Son and of the Holy Spirit, teaching them to observe everything I have commanded you. And remember, I am with you always, to the end of the age.'" (Matthew 28:18–20, CSB)

- Who gave the Great Commission found in Matthew 28:18–20?

Jesus gave the Great Commission to his disciples as their mission and purpose in life. For the Christian, life should be about making disciples.

Why do Christians make disciples? Because Jesus tells us to.

Ask your disciple, what is your life's purpose? Does that purpose fit in with the Great Commission?

- Underline the instructions given in Matthew 28:18–20.

Jesus instructs us to make disciples of all nations, baptizing them in the name of the Father and of the Son and of the Holy Spirit, teaching them to observe everything he has commanded them. Whether a Christ follower is at home or abroad, they must be obedient in making disciples.

- What does it mean to *make disciples of all nations*?

Make disciples of all nations in the Great Commission tells disciples that they must be constantly reduplicating. Disciples are to share the faith that was given to them by teaching others about Jesus and how to follow him. The process of making disciples is not limited in scope—it includes people of every nation, tribe, and tongue.

- What does it mean to *baptize them in the name of the Father and of the Son and of the Holy Spirit*?

Baptize them in the name of the Father and of the Son and of the Holy Spirit in the Great Commission tells disciples that they must intentionally call people to follow the one true God.

- What does it mean to *teach them to observe everything I have commanded you*?

Teach them to observe everything I have commanded you in the Great Commission tells disciples that they must be doers of the Word and teach others how to follow God's Word.

What is Discipleship?

What you have heard from me in the presence of many witnesses, commit to faithful men who will be able to teach others also. (2 Timothy 2:2, CSB)

- What does 2 Timothy 2:2 tell you about discipleship?

> **What is discipleship?**
>
> Discipleship is one Christian sharing what the Christian life is all about. Discipleship consists of the disciple-maker transferring knowledge as well as lifestyle to the disciple.

How Do You Identify Someone to Disciple?

You find someone who is **F.A.T.** I do not mean that he or she is overweight. But he or she needs to be hungry, hungry to grow in the Lord. Here are three characteristics that have helped me find good disciples.

- **Faithful** - The person you choose to disciple may not be a believer when you begin to disciple him or her, but they must be committed to the task. If you try to disciple a person who is not faithful to the task, discipleship will not happen no matter how hard you try.

- **Available** - Availability is hard. People are always so busy. That is why availability is a key component when looking for someone to disciple. If a person does not have the time to invest in his or her spiritual growth, discipleship will not happen.

- **Teachable** - You cannot teach someone who knows it all. While it may be tempting to pick a disciple who has all the answers, make sure that person is teachable. The purpose of discipleship is to help him or her grow in the Lord.

> **How do you identify someone who to disciple? Look for the characteristics of a F.A.T. disciple.**
>
> Disciple-maker, are there any characteristics that you would add to this list?
>
> This is a time for you to encourage your disciple by telling of his or her potential to serve the Lord and tell them why you chose him or her for discipleship.

Are You Ready to Make Disciples?

Discuss with your discipleship partner any issues that would keep you from discipling someone else.

Think through the people you know. Identify three people who would benefit from being discipled.

Person 1. _____

Person 2. _____

Person 3. _____

_____

Pray together over those you have identified and ask God for opportunities to make disciples.

Week 5 Day 1 – WHAT IS THE BIG DEAL ABOUT DISCIPLESHIP?

Review:
Romans 6:23
2 Corinthians 5:17
Ephesians 1:7
Galatians 4:4–5
1 Corinthians 12:13
John 13:34–35
Hebrews 10:24–25

Read - 2 Timothy 2:2
What you have heard from me in the presence of many witnesses, commit to faithful men who will be able to teach others also. (2 Timothy 2:2, CSB)

Reflect - What does this verse tell you...
about God?

about yourself?

about God's grace?

Respond - Is there something that you need to...
know about?

share or do?

praise God for?

pray over?

Week 5 Day 2 – WHAT IS THE BIG DEAL ABOUT DISCIPLESHIP?

Review:

Romans 6:23
2 Corinthians 5:17
Ephesians 1:7
Galatians 4:4–5
1 Corinthians 12:13
John 13:34–35
Hebrews 10:24–25

Write - 2 Timothy 2:2

Read - Luke 10:1–11

"After this, the Lord appointed seventy-two others, and he sent them ahead of him in pairs to every town and place where he himself was about to go. He told them, "The harvest is abundant, but the workers are few. Therefore, pray to the Lord of the harvest to send out workers into his harvest. Now go; I'm sending you out like lambs among wolves. Don't carry a money-bag, traveling bag, or sandals; don't greet anyone along the road. Whatever house you enter, first say, 'Peace to this household.' If a person of peace is there, your peace will rest on him; but if not, it will return to you. Remain in the same house, eating and drinking what they offer, for the worker is worthy of his wages. Don't move from house to house. When you enter any town, and they welcome you, eat the things set before you. Heal the sick who are there, and tell them, 'The kingdom of God has come near you.' When you enter any town, and they don't welcome you, go out into its streets and say, 'We are wiping off even the dust of your town that clings to our feet as a witness against you. Know this for certain: The kingdom of God has come near.'"
(Luke 10:1–11, CSB)

Reflect - What does this verse tell you...

about God?

----

about yourself?

----

about God's grace?

Respond - Is there something that you need to...

know about?

----

share or do?

----

praise God for?

----

pray over?

Week 5 Day 3 – WHAT IS THE BIG DEAL ABOUT DISCIPLESHIP?

Review:
> Romans 6:23
> 2 Corinthians 5:17
> Ephesians 1:7
> Galatians 4:4–5
> 1 Corinthians 12:13
> John 13:34–35
> Hebrews 10:24–25

Write - 2 Timothy 2:2

Read - Matthew 16:24–25

"Then Jesus said to his disciples, "If anyone wants to follow after me, let him deny himself, take up his cross, and follow me. For whoever wants to save his life will lose it, but whoever loses his life because of me will find it." (Matthew 16:24–25, CSB)

Reflect - What does this verse tell you...
about God?

----

about yourself?

----

about God's grace?

Respond - Is there something that you need to...

know about?

share or do?

praise God for?

pray over?

Week 5 Day 4 – WHAT IS THE BIG DEAL ABOUT DISCIPLESHIP?

Review:

Romans 6:23
2 Corinthians 5:17
Ephesians 1:7
Galatians 4:4–5
1 Corinthians 12:13
John 13:34–35
Hebrews 10:24–25

Write - 2 Timothy 2:2

Read - Acts 2:42–47

"They devoted themselves to the apostles' teaching, to the fellowship, to the breaking of bread, and to prayer. Everyone was filled with awe, and many wonders and signs were being performed through the apostles. Now all the believers were together and held all things in common. They sold their possessions and property and distributed the proceeds to all, as any had need. Every day they devoted themselves to meeting together in the temple, and broke bread from house to house. They ate their food with joyful and sincere hearts, praising God and enjoying the favor of all the people. Every day the Lord added to their number those who were being saved." (Acts 2:42–47, CSB)

Reflect - What does this verse tell you...

about God?

_____

_____

about yourself?

_____

_____

about God's grace?

_____

_____

Respond - Is there something that you need to...

know about?

_____

_____

share or do?

_____

_____

praise God for?

_____

_____

pray over?

_____

_____

Week 5 Day 5 – WHAT IS THE BIG DEAL ABOUT DISCIPLESHIP?

Review:

Romans 6:23
2 Corinthians 5:17
Ephesians 1:7
Galatians 4:4–5
1 Corinthians 12:13
John 13:34–35
Hebrews 10:24–25

Write - 2 Timothy 2:2

Read - Luke 14:25–35

"Now great crowds were traveling with him. So he turned and said to them: "If anyone comes to me and does not hate his own father and mother, wife and children, brothers and sisters—yes, and even his own life—he cannot be my disciple. Whoever does not bear his own cross and come after me cannot be my disciple. "For which of you, wanting to build a tower, doesn't first sit down and calculate the cost to see if he has enough to complete it? Otherwise, after he has laid the foundation and cannot finish it, all the onlookers will begin to ridicule him, saying, 'This man started to build and wasn't able to finish.' "Or what king, going to war against another king, will not first sit down and decide if he is able with ten thousand to oppose the one who comes against him with twenty thousand? If not, while the other is still far off, he sends a delegation and asks for terms of peace. In the same way, therefore, every one of you who does not renounce all his possessions cannot be my disciple. "Now, salt is good, but if salt should lose its taste, how will it be made salty? It isn't fit for the soil or for the manure pile; they throw it out. Let anyone who has ears to hear listen."" (Luke 14:25–35, CSB)

Reflect - What does this verse tell you...

about God?

---

about yourself?

---

about God's grace?

Respond - Is there something that you need to...

know about?

---

share or do?

---

praise God for?

---

pray over?

Week 5 Day 6 – WHAT IS THE BIG DEAL ABOUT DISCIPLESHIP?

Review:

> Romans 6:23
> 2 Corinthians 5:17
> Ephesians 1:7
> Galatians 4:4–5
> 1 Corinthians 12:13
> John 13:34–35
> Hebrews 10:24–25

Write - 2 Timothy 2:2

Read- John 15:1–8

"I am the true vine, and my Father is the gardener. Every branch in me that does not produce fruit he removes, and he prunes every branch that produces fruit so that it will produce more fruit. You are already clean because of the word I have spoken to you. Remain in me, and I in you. Just as a branch is unable to produce fruit by itself unless it remains on the vine, neither can you unless you remain in me. I am the vine; you are the branches. The one who remains in me and I in him produces much fruit, because you can do nothing without me. If anyone does not remain in me, he is thrown aside like a branch and he withers. They gather them, throw them into the fire, and they are burned. If you remain in me and my words remain in you, ask whatever you want and it will be done for you. My Father is glorified by this: that you produce much fruit and prove to be my disciples."
(John 15:1–8, CSB)

Reflect - What does this verse tell you...
about God?

about yourself?

about God's grace?

Respond - Is there something that you need to...
know about?

share or do?

praise God for?

pray over?

Week 5 Day 7– WHAT IS THE BIG DEAL ABOUT DISCIPLESHIP?

Review:
Romans 6:23
2 Corinthians 5:17
Ephesians 1:7
Galatians 4:4–5
1 Corinthians 12:13
John 13:34–35
Hebrews 10:24–25

Write - 2 Timothy 2:2

Sermon Notes
Speaker:

Date:

Text:

SESSION 6 – WHAT IS THE CHRISTIAN MISSION?

Week six is about the Christian mission. There are many opinions on what it means to be a Christian. But to actually be a Christian, you must follow Christ. Therefore, the mission of a Christian is to do the things that Jesus did and follow his direction in daily life. This session will discuss the ministry of Jesus, his disciples, and the early church to see how their mission can become every Christian's mission.

Disciple-maker,
1) Review the Scripture memory from the previous weeks.
2) Review last week's daily devotionals and sermon notes.
3) Pray over the meeting with your disciple before starting.
4) Have your disciples circle or highlight key phrases of the Scriptures in their book and discuss the concepts as found in the Scriptures with your disciple.

What was Jesus's Mission?

"For the Son of Man has come to seek and to save the lost." (Luke 19:10, CSB)

- Who is *the Son of Man*?

- What did *the Son of Man* come to do?

What was Jesus' mission? To seek out those who are lost.

The mission of Jesus was to save sinners and in doing so bring God glory. If this was Jesus' mission, our mission should be the same. We, as Christians, should be on a mission to seek and save the lost.

What was Jesus's Feeling toward those who were Lost and are Found?

"So he told them this parable: 'What man among you, who has a hundred sheep and loses one of them, does not leave the ninety-nine in the open field and go after the lost one until he finds it?

When he has found it, he joyfully puts it on his shoulders, and coming home, he calls his friends and neighbors together, saying to them, 'Rejoice with me, because I have found my lost sheep!' I tell you, in the same way, there will be more joy in heaven over one sinner who repents than over ninety-nine righteous people who don't need repentance.'" (Luke 15:3–7, CSB)

- Who is the shepherd in the parable?

- Who are the sheep in the parable?

- What does the shepherd do when he loses one of his sheep?

- What does the shepherd do when he finds his lost sheep?

- What is this parable describing?

What was Jesus's feeling toward those who were lost and are found? Jesus rejoiced for those lost who are found!

Rejoicing should be our attitude when a lost person repents of sins and comes into a relationship with Jesus.

What did Jesus Send his Disciples to Do?

"Jesus said to them again, 'Peace be with you. As the Father has sent me, I also send you.' After saying this, he breathed on them and said, 'Receive the Holy Spirit. If you forgive the sins of any, they are forgiven them; if you retain the sins of any, they are retained.'" (John 20:21–23, CSB)

- In this passage, Jesus sent his disciples out. What were his disciples supposed to do from this point on?
- Jesus gave them something to help them with their mission to reach the lost. What is that help?

What did Jesus send his disciples to do? Jesus sent his disciples to do as He had done.

Just as the Heavenly Father sent Jesus to seek and save sinners, Jesus sent his followers to seek and save sinners. Jesus gave his followers a great help when he sent them. He gave them the Holy Spirit who would guide them in this mission and work with them to accomplish the task.

Christians today have the same command. We too are sent out into the world with the aid of the Holy Spirit to seek out the lost as Jesus did and present salvation to them.

What was the Mission of the Early Church?

"Jesus came near and said to them, 'All authority has been given to me in heaven and on earth. Go, therefore, and make disciples of all nations, baptizing them in the name of the Father and of the Son and of the Holy Spirit, teaching them to observe everything I have commanded you. And remember, I am with you always, to the end of the age.'" (Matthew 28:18–20, CSB)

"Then he said to them, 'Go into all the world and preach the gospel to all creation.'" (Mark 16:15, CSB)

- Both of these passages record Jesus' instructions to the early church. In your own words, write what you think Jesus was telling the church to do.

Disciple-maker, help your disciple understand the mission of the church to share the gospel. Share the time in which you came to understand this truth.

Are You Ready to Be a Christian on Mission?

Discuss with your discipleship partner anything that would hold you back from being on mission to share the gospel.

Do you have any questions about sharing the gospel with the lost?

Spend a few moments and think through the people you know. Identify three people who need to hear the gospel.

Person 1.
_____

_____
Person 2.
_____

_____
Person 3.
_____

_____

Spend some time with your discipleship partner praying for these people. Ask God to give them salvation. Ask God to give you opportunities to share the gospel with them. Ask God for boldness as you go on mission.

Week 6 Day 1 – WHAT IS THE CHRISTIAN MISSION?

Review:
> Romans 6:23
> 2 Corinthians 5:17
> Ephesians 1:7
> Galatians 4:4–5
> 1 Corinthians 12:13
> John 13:34–35
> Hebrews 10:24–25
> 2 Timothy 2:2

Read - Matthew 28:18–20

"Jesus came near and said to them, 'All authority has been given to me in heaven and on earth. Go, therefore, and make disciples of all nations, baptizing them in the name of the Father and of the Son and of the Holy Spirit, teaching them to observe everything I have commanded you. And remember, I am with you always, to the end of the age.'" (Matthew 28:18–20, CSB)

Reflect - What does this verse tell you...
about God?

about yourself?

about God's grace?

Respond - Is there something that you need to...

know about?

- -

- -

- -

share or do?

- -

- -

praise God for?

- -

- -

pray over?

- -

- -

Week 6 Day 2 – WHAT IS THE CHRISTIAN MISSION?

Review:

Romans 6:23
2 Corinthians 5:17
Ephesians 1:7
Galatians 4:4–5
1 Corinthians 12:13
John 13:34–35
Hebrews 10:24–25
2 Timothy 2:2

Write - Matthew 28:18–20

Read - Genesis 3:15

"I will put hostility between you and the woman, and between your offspring and her offspring. He will strike your head, and you will strike his heel." (Genesis 3:15, CSB)

Reflect - What does this verse tell you...

about God?

----

about yourself?

----

about God's grace?

Respond - Is there something that you need to...
know about?

_____

_____

_____

share or do?

_____

_____

praise God for?

_____

_____

pray over?

_____

_____

_____

Week 6 Day 3 – WHAT IS THE CHRISTIAN MISSION?

Review:
    Romans 6:23
    2 Corinthians 5:17
    Ephesians 1:7
    Galatians 4:4–5
    1 Corinthians 12:13
    John 13:34–35
    Hebrews 10:24–25
    2 Timothy 2:2

Write - Matthew 28:18–20

Read - Luke 19:10
"For the Son of Man has come to seek and to save the lost."
(Luke 19:10, CSB)

Reflect - What does this verse tell you...
about God?

----

about yourself?

----

about God's grace?

Respond - Is there something that you need to...

know about?

----

share or do?

----

praise God for?

----

pray over?

Week 6 Day 4 – WHAT IS THE CHRISTIAN MISSION?

Review:
Romans 6:23
2 Corinthians 5:17
Ephesians 1:7
Galatians 4:4–5
1 Corinthians 12:13
John 13:34–35
Hebrews 10:24–25
2 Timothy 2:2

Write - Matthew 28:18–20

Read - 2 Timothy 4:5
"But as for you, exercise self-control in everything, endure hardship, do the work of an evangelist, fulfill your ministry." (2 Timothy 4:5, CSB)

Reflect - What does this verse tell you...
about God?

----

about yourself?

----

about God's grace?

Respond - Is there something that you need to...

know about?

---

share or do?

---

praise God for?

---

pray over?

Week 6 Day 5 – WHAT IS THE CHRISTIAN MISSION?

Review:

Romans 6:23

2 Corinthians 5:17

Ephesians 1:7

Galatians 4:4–5

1 Corinthians 12:13

John 13:34–35

Hebrews 10:24–25

2 Timothy 2:2

Write - Matthew 28:18–20

Read - Ephesians 4:11–12

"And he himself gave some to be apostles, some prophets, some evangelists, some pastors and teachers, equipping the saints for the work of ministry, to build up the body of Christ." (Ephesians 4:11–12, CSB)

Reflect - What does this verse tell you...

about God?

----

about yourself?

----

about God's grace?

Respond - Is there something that you need to...

know about?

----

share or do?

----

praise God for?

----

pray over?

Week 6 Day 6 – WHAT IS THE CHRISTIAN MISSION?

Review:

Romans 6:23
2 Corinthians 5:17
Ephesians 1:7
Galatians 4:4–5
1 Corinthians 12:13
John 13:34–35
Hebrews 10:24–25
2 Timothy 2:2

Write - Matthew 28:18–20

Read- 1 Corinthians 15:3–8

"For I passed on to you as most important what I also received: that Christ died for our sins according to the Scriptures, that he was buried, that he was raised on the third day according to the Scriptures, and that he appeared to Cephas, then to the Twelve. Then he appeared to over five hundred brothers and sisters at one time; most of them are still alive, but some have fallen asleep. Then he appeared to James, then to all the apostles. Last of all, as to one born at the wrong time, he also appeared to me." (1 Corinthians 15:3–8, CSB)

Reflect - What does this verse tell you...
about God?

----

about yourself?

----

about God's grace?

Respond - Is there something that you need to...
know about?

----

share or do?

----

praise God for?

----

pray over?

Week 6 Day 7– WHAT IS THE CHRISTIAN MISSION?

Review:
>Romans 6:23
>2 Corinthians 5:17
>Ephesians 1:7
>Galatians 4:4–5
>1 Corinthians 12:13
>John 13:34–35
>Hebrews 10:24–25
>2 Timothy 2:2

Write - Matthew 28:18–20

Sermon Notes
Speaker:

Date:

Text:

SESSION 7 – WHAT COMES NEXT?

YOU MADE IT!

This is the final session of this discipleship material. BUT we are not done yet. We have to put these things into practice. These past 6 weeks have been a journey in understanding the Scripture more and applying it to our everyday life. That being said, we need to evaluate all that we have learned and take the necessary action steps. Take some time to answer the following questions with your discipleship partner.

Did you receive Jesus as your Lord and Savior over the course of the discipleship sessions?

Did you gain a better understanding of what it means to be saved over the course of the discipleship sessions?

Did you get baptized or gain a better understanding of baptism over the course of the discipleship sessions?

Did you find a local church family or get a better understanding of what it means to be a church member over the course of the discipleship sessions?

Did you do all off the daily devotions for...

(Check off the weeks you completed)

- o Week 1
- o Week 2
- o Week 3
- o Week 4
- o Week 5
- o Week 6

Disciple-maker, encourage your disciple in what they have done and cover any questions they may have about the daily devotions.

Did you memorize all of the Scriptures?

(Check off the Scriptures you memorized)

- o Romans 6:23
- o 2 Corinthians 5:17
- o Ephesians 1:7
- o Galatians 4:4–5
- o 1 Corinthians 12:13
- o John 13:34–35
- o Hebrews 10:24–25
- o 2 Timothy 2:2
- o Matthew 28:18–20

Disciple-maker, encourage your disciple in the Scriptures they have memorized. Scripture memory can be difficult for people, so make sure to rejoice in what was accomplished.

Did you ask someone to do discipleship with you over the course of the sessions?

Person 1.

Person 2.

Person 3.

Did you share the Gospel with someone over the course of the sessions?

Person 1.

Person 2.

Person 3.

Wow! That is a lot of work accomplished! Congratulations on all your spiritual progress!

As you go out into the world, my hope for you is that you do not stop here.

My hope for you is that you continue to pursue God through the study of His Word. I have found discipleship to be more of a journey than a program. Discipleship lasts a lifetime. As we get older, God teaches us more, faith grows, and we mature in the faith. My hope is that this would be the beginning and that you continue to grow in Christ and follow Him closer.

My hope for you is that God would use you greatly to seek and save the lost and make disciples of all nations. Over the course of my life, God has brought new people into my life that He wanted me to invest in. God does this through different seasons of life. My hope is that you would be aware of what God is doing around you and be aware of those who He wants you to invest in. I also hope that you would be a disciple-maker for Him to use to reach the world.

APPENDIX

What Is the Bible?

1. **The Bible Is God's Word.**
   "All Scripture is inspired by God and is profitable for teaching, for rebuking, for correcting, for training in righteousness." (2 Timothy 3:16, CSB)

   The Bible is God's decree and personal address to humanity, spoken through the lips and writings of men. Scripture provides God's instructions and laws for mankind as well as addresses mankind's needs for salvation and relationship with God. Many pastors have illustrated this by making the statement, "If you want to know the will of God, open your Bible. If you want to hear God speak to you, read your Bible out loud." While the illustration is cute, it works to show us that when we open God's Word we expect to hear from him.

2. **The Bible Is How Christians Know God.**
   "Jesus answered, 'If anyone loves me, he will keep my word. My Father will love him, and we will come to him and make our home with him. The one who doesn't love me will not keep my words. The word that you hear is not mine but is from the Father who sent me.'" (John 14:23–24, CSB)

   The Bible is God's revelation of himself to mankind. One of the best ways to know God and know about God is through His Word. The Word of God is the supreme standard by which we get to know God. The Word of God is priceless for the Christian and the love of the Word is one of the defining fruits of the Christian life.

3. **The Bible Is How Christians Know God's Will.**
   "This book of instruction must not depart from your mouth; you are to meditate on it day and night so that you may carefully observe everything written in it. For then you will prosper and succeed in whatever you do." (Joshua 1:8, CSB)

   The Bible is God's instruction for Christians. God's Word provides real and applicable insights into all of creation. If a person has a question about life or a situation they are facing, they should read their Scriptures. Christians hold the Bible dear as their guide for life.

Tips for Memorizing Scripture

1. **Understand the context.** Scripture memory is easier when you understand why you are learning the Scripture. We do not do things without reason. So ask yourself, why am I memorizing this Scripture?

2. **Meditate on the Scripture.** Think about it when you are still and your mind is quiet. Recite it out loud or in your head. When you lay your head down at night, recite the words in your thoughts while going to sleep.

3. **Pair the Scripture with the reference.** You want to remember where you found that Scripture you memorized when you quote it. When you recite the verse, recite the reference as well. When you create flash cards, write down the reference with the verse and read them together.

4. **Say the Scripture out loud.** Read the Scripture out loud over and over. Doing this allows you to hear them as you say them and it will help with memorizing them.

5. **Write the Scripture out.** One of the easiest ways to memorize Scripture is to write it out. Try it. Write it out ten to twenty times. It is hard at first and then you got it.

6. **Refresh often.** If you do not continually work to refresh your Scripture memory, you will forget them. When you memorize your weekly Scripture make sure that you not only work to memorize your new Scripture, but you refresh the Scriptures that you have already memorized, cementing them into your long-term memory.

About the Contributors

Anthony Svajda –General Editor and Contributor
Sessions 1, 3, 5, 6, 7, and Appendix

Anthony Svajda (Southwestern Baptist Theological Seminary, Ph.D.) has served many different ministry roles in small and large churches. Currently, he is serving as the lead pastor of Harvey Baptist Church in Stephenville, Texas. He is married to Kristen and they have two children.

David Norman - Contributor
Session 2

David G. Norman, Jr. (Southwestern Baptist Theological Seminary, Ph.D.) has served in a number of roles and contexts. More recently, he has trained ministers of the Gospel as an adjunct professor at Southwestern Baptist Theological Seminary, Midwestern Baptist Theological Seminary, and California Baptist University Online. David is married to Krista and they have five children.

Sean Wegner - Contributor
Session 4

Sean M. Wegener (Southwestern Baptist Theological Seminary, M.Div.) serves as the pastor of Summerville First Baptist in Summerville, Georgia and is a Ph.D. candidate at Southwestern Baptist Theological Seminary. He is married to Danielle and they have four boys.